Sober Curious Drinks

Drinks

NON-ALCOHOLIC COCKTAIL RECIPES THAT
ARE EASY TO MAKE, TASTE DELICIOUS,
AND WON'T LEAVE YOU FEELING HANGOVER

BY STELLA ROSE WILDER

Cheers to you—and life beyond alcohol. May each sip bring you closer to your true self and remind you that you are never alone on this journey.

Contents

Chapter 1:

The Sober Curious
Movement

SOBER CURIOUS DRINKS

Welcome to the world of non-alcoholic mixology! In recent years, a remarkable cultural shift has taken place, giving rise to a movement known as "sober curious." The sober curious movement is a growing community of individuals choosing to reevaluate their relationship with alcohol and explore a life of sobriety or moderation. Rather than accepting alcohol as a societal norm, they are embracing a more mindful and intentional approach to drinking.

I first learned about the term "sober curious" while doom scrolling Tik Tok. While avoiding sleep, delicious non-alcoholic cocktail recipes would pop up on my page in-between funny cats and prank phone call videos. I was inspired to learn more.

Ruby Warrington is a pioneer in the sober curious movement helping people live a more connected life through her podcast, "Sober Curious," and book, "*Sober Curious: The Blissful Sleep, Greater Focus, Limited Presence, and Deep Connection Awaiting Us All on the Other Side of Alcohol.*"

By accepting sobriety or moderating alcohol intake, people in the sober curious movement are discovering many benefits. From improved physical health to mental clarity, enhanced creativity to deeper connections, the decision to step away from alcohol can transform every aspect of life. Removing alcohol from the equation allows individuals to discover new passions, unlock hidden potential, and cultivate a more authentic sense of self.

Whether you're considering a break from alcohol, experimenting with sobriety, or simply looking for delicious alcohol-free alternatives to wind down your day, this book will guide you through creating a vibrant world of flavors, textures, and experiences that will ensure you don't miss the booze in your drink.

With this collection of non-alcoholic cocktail recipes, we aim to provide you with a diverse range of options inspired by classic cocktails but devoid of alcohol. Each recipe captures the essence, complexity, and enjoyment of traditional cocktails while offering unique twists and innovative flavor combinations.

Whether you're hosting a party, enjoying a relaxing evening at home, or looking for the perfect drink to pair with a special meal, this book will equip you with the knowledge, techniques, and inspiration to become a master of the art of non-alcoholic mixology. Get ready to embark on a journey of tantalizing tastes, creative concoctions, and delightful discoveries.

So, raise your glass to a vibrant and fulfilling life without alcohol on your sober curious journey as we explore the art of non-alcoholic mixology!

Chapter 2:

Stocking Your Mocktail Bar

Non-alcoholic cocktails, also known as mocktails, have a rich and fascinating history that dates back centuries. While the term "mocktail" was coined in the 20th century, alcohol-free specialty drinks have existed for much longer. In ancient times, various cultures created herbal infusions, fruit punches, and botanical concoctions enjoyed as refreshing alternatives to alcoholic drinks.

During the era of Prohibition in the United States (1920-1933), the demand for creative non-alcoholic beverages skyrocketed. Bartenders and mixologists began crafting elaborate mocktails to satisfy the thirst of those who could not legally consume alcohol. These mocktails featured complex flavor profiles, intricate garnishes, and innovative techniques that continue to inspire the world of non-alcoholic mixology today.

In recent years, the resurgence of mocktails has been fueled by the sober curious movement and the growing demand for alcohol-free options. Today, mocktails have evolved into a sophisticated art form, with talented mixologists worldwide creating innovative and delectable concoctions that rival their alcoholic counterparts.

Let's explore the essential ingredients and tools to create a delicious mocktail.

Mocktail Base Ingredients:

To create enticing non-alcoholic cocktails, it's essential to have a selection of key ingredients and substitutes that mimic the flavors, aromas, and textures associated with alcoholic beverages. Some commonly used ingredients and substitutes include:

- Fresh fruits and juices: Citrus fruits like lemons, limes, and oranges are staples in non-alcoholic mixology. They provide acidity, brightness, and a burst of refreshing flavor. Other fruits like berries, watermelon, pineapple, and mango can be muddled, pureed, or juiced to add sweetness and complexity.

- Herbs and botanicals: Ingredients such as mint, basil, rosemary, lavender, and thyme bring herbaceous and aromatic notes to mocktails. They can be muddled, infused in syrups, or used as garnishes to enhance the flavor profile.

- Syrups, shrubs, and bitters: Homemade or store-bought syrups—such as simple syrup or flavored syrups—and fruit-based shrubs add depth, sweetness, and complexity to mocktails. Non-alcoholic bitters, made from botanical extracts and spices, provide a nuanced flavor profile to drinks.

- Sparkling water and sodas: Carbonated beverages like club soda, tonic water, ginger ale, and cola can add effervescence and texture to mocktails. They also serve as excellent mixers and provide a refreshing fizz.

- Non-alcoholic spirits (optional): These are distilled beverages that undergo the same production process as their alcoholic counterparts but have the alcohol content removed. Examples include non-alcoholic gin, whiskey, rum, and tequila, which provide a familiar taste profile without the intoxicating effects. Non-alcoholic spirits are unnecessary to create refreshing mocktails and have been omitted from this book to keep the recipes simple and accessible for beginners, but each recipe can easily accommodate their addition.

Mocktail Mixology Tools:

It's helpful to have a few essential tools to elevate your non-alcoholic mixology skills. These include:

Cocktail shaker: A shaker is useful for vigorously mixing ingredients, infusing flavors, and creating a frothy texture in certain drinks.

Muddler: This tool is used to crush fruits, herbs, and spices to release their essential oils and flavors.

Mixing glass and bar spoon: A mixing glass is ideal for gently stirring ingredients to ensure proper blending without excessive dilution. A long bar spoon is used for stirring and layering ingredients.

Strainer: A strainer is essential for separating solid ingredients, such as fruit pulp or herbs, from the liquid when pouring the mocktail into a glass (note: many cocktail shakers have a built-in strainer).

Jigger or measuring tools: Accurate measurements are essential in mixology. A jigger or measuring tool to measure ounces ensures consistency and flavor balance.

Glassware: Depending on the types of mocktails you wish to create, a variety of glassware—like rocks glasses, highball glasses, martini glasses, and coupe glasses—can be used to serve your creations.

By familiarizing yourself with these key ingredients and necessary tools, you'll be well-prepared to dive into the captivating world of non-alcoholic mixology and create extraordinary mocktails that tantalize the taste buds and delight the senses.

Chapter 3:

Mocktail Mixology
Techniques and Tips

In non-alcoholic mixology, mastering essential techniques and learning valuable tips can elevate your drink-making skills to new heights. This chapter aims to help you in honing your craft and becoming a skilled non-alcoholic mixologist. Whether you're a beginner or an experienced bartender, these tips will enhance your ability to create delicious and visually stunning alcohol-free beverages.

Muddling and infusing flavors:

Muddling is a fundamental technique in non-alcoholic mixology that involves gently crushing ingredients to release their flavors and aromas. Here are some tips for effective muddling and infusing:

- Use a sturdy muddler: Choose a muddler with a flat, textured end to efficiently extract flavors without damaging the ingredients.

- Gentle pressure: Apply gentle pressure while muddling to avoid over-extracting bitterness from certain ingredients like citrus peels or herbs.

- Muddle in a cocktail shaker or mixing glass: Place the ingredients at the bottom of the shaker or mixing glass and gently press and twist with the muddler to release the desired flavors.

- Experiment with infusions: Besides muddling, you can create flavorful infusions by combining ingredients with water, tea, or other liquids and letting them sit to extract the flavors. For example, infusing cucumber slices in water or rosemary in simple syrup can add unique tastes to your mocktails.

Creating flavorful syrups and shrubs:

Syrups and shrubs are essential components of non-alcoholic mixology, providing sweetness, depth, and complexity to your mocktails. Here's how to create flavorful syrups and shrubs:

- Simple syrup: Combine equal parts water and sugar in a saucepan. Heat over medium heat, stirring until the sugar dissolves, then allow the syrup to cool before mixing into mocktails.

- Flavored syrups: Experiment with different flavors by adding fruits, herbs, or spices to the simple syrup mixture while heating. Allow the ingredients to steep for a few minutes before straining to create a wide range of flavored syrups. Chapter 4 teaches you how to make vanilla, lavender, rosemary, elderflower, and rose infused simple syrups.

- Shrubs: Shrubs are vinegar-based syrups that add tanginess and complexity to mocktails. Combine equal parts fruit, sugar, and vinegar (apple cider vinegar or balsamic vinegar work well) in a jar. Let the ingredients sit in the refrigerator for a few days, shaking occasionally, to allow the flavors to meld. Strain before using. Chapter 12 teaches you how to make fruity and tangy shrub bases, while Chapter 13 provides delicious mocktail recipes using your homemade shrubs.

Balancing acidity and sweetness:

Achieving the perfect balance between acidity and sweetness is crucial in non-alcoholic mixology. Consider the following tips:

- Citrus juices: Use fresh-squeezed citrus juices like lemon, lime, or grapefruit to add acidity and brightness. Taste as you go and adjust the amount based on personal preference.

- Sweeteners: Experiment with different sweeteners like simple syrup, agave nectar, honey, or maple syrup. Start with small amounts and gradually increase until the desired sweetness is achieved.

- Acid balancing: If a mocktail is too tart, balance the acidity by adding a touch of sweetness. Conversely, if it's overly sweet, add a splash of citrus juice or a dash of vinegar to bring out the tartness.

Garnishing and presentation ideas:

Garnishing and presentation play a significant role in enhancing the visual appeal and overall experience of your mocktails. Consider the following suggestions:

- Fresh herbs and citrus twists: Add a mint sprig, a lemon or lime peel twist, or a small cluster of berries as garnishes. These elements not only add visual appeal but also contribute to the aroma and flavor of the mocktail.

- Edible flowers: Delicate edible flowers, such as pansies or violets, can elevate the aesthetics of your mocktails. Ensure any plants used are pesticide-free and edible before using them as garnishes.

- Creative glassware: Choose glassware that complements the style of your mocktail. To enhance the presentation, experiment with different shapes and sizes, such as coupe glasses, mason jars, or decorative tumblers.

- Ice and texture: Play with different ice shapes, such as large cubes or crushed ice, to add texture and visual interest. You can also experiment with frozen fruit or herb-infused ice cubes to bring extra flavor and aesthetics.

Remember, garnishing is an opportunity to showcase your creativity and make your mocktails visually appealing. Let your imagination run wild and have fun with it!

By mastering these essential techniques, you'll be well on your way to creating beautifully balanced, flavorful, and visually captivating non-alcoholic cocktails. By feeling confident in your abilities as a mixologist, you'll be more likely to enjoy the process of exploring new ingredients, experimenting with flavors, and delighting in the art of mocktail creation.

Now, let's get started with our recipes!

Chapter 4:

Simple Syrup Recipes
and Infusions

SOBER CURIOUS DRINKS

Simple syrups are a fundamental ingredient in mocktails and cocktails alike. They are a mixture of equal parts sugar and water, heated until the sugar fully dissolves, creating a sweet, liquid syrup. Simple syrups are used to add sweetness, balance flavors, and enhance the overall taste of beverages.

In mocktails, simple syrups are a versatile base for creating customized flavors. They can be infused with various ingredients like herbs, fruits, spices, or even floral essences to add complexity and depth to the drink. The process of infusing the syrup involves steeping the desired ingredient in the hot syrup, allowing the flavors to meld over time.

When making a mocktail, you can add simple syrup to your drink as a sweetener. Start with a small amount and adjust to taste, as some mocktails may require more or less sweetness depending on the other ingredients used and personal preference. Stir the mocktail well to ensure the simple syrup is thoroughly incorporated.

Simple syrups offer endless possibilities for customizing mocktails. They allow you to experiment and create unique combinations that suit your taste preferences. So, have fun exploring different flavors and infusions to elevate your mocktail creations.

Basic Simple Syrup

Simple syrup is a versatile way to add sweetness to your drinks. It's incredibly easy to make by following these steps:

 **INGREDIENTS**

- 1 cup granulated sugar
- 1 cup water

 **DIRECTIONS**

1. In a saucepan, combine equal parts sugar and water. You can adjust the quantities for a batch of any size while maintaining a 1:1 ratio.
2. Place the saucepan over medium heat and stir continuously until the sugar completely dissolves, and the mixture appears clear.
3. Once the sugar has dissolved, remove the saucepan from the heat. Allow the simple syrup to cool to room temperature.
4. Once the syrup has cooled, transfer it to a clean, airtight container, such as a glass bottle or jar. You can also use a squeeze bottle for easier dispensing.
5. Label the container with the date of preparation, as simple syrup can typically be stored in the refrigerator for up to one month.

That's it! Your homemade simple syrup is ready to use. Enjoy the simplicity and convenience of having homemade simple syrup on hand for all your drink creations.

Vanilla Simple Syrup

To infuse the delightful essence of vanilla into simple syrup, you can follow these easy steps:

 INGREDIENTS

- 1 cup water
- 1 cup granulated sugar

- 1 vanilla bean or 1 tablespoon pure vanilla extract

 DIRECTIONS

1. In a saucepan, combine water and sugar over medium heat. Stir until the sugar has completely dissolved.
2. If using a vanilla bean, split it lengthwise and scrape out the seeds. Add both the scraped-out seeds and the empty vanilla bean pod to the saucepan. If using vanilla extract, skip this step.
3. Bring the mixture to a gentle simmer, stirring occasionally to ensure the sugar is fully dissolved and the vanilla flavors infuse the syrup.
4. Allow the mixture to simmer for about 5 minutes. This will create a

fragrant and rich vanilla simple syrup.

5.   After simmering, remove the saucepan from the heat and let the vanilla-infused syrup cool to room temperature. This will give the flavors time to meld and develop.

6.   Once cooled, remove the vanilla bean pod, if used, and strain the syrup through a fine-mesh sieve or cheesecloth to remove any impurities.

7.   If you opted for vanilla extract instead of a vanilla bean, stir in 1 tablespoon of pure vanilla extract once the syrup has cooled.

8.   Transfer the vanilla-infused simple syrup to a clean, airtight container, such as a glass bottle or jar, and store it in the refrigerator for up to 1 month.

Now you have your homemade vanilla-infused simple syrup ready to add a touch of sweet vanilla goodness to your beverages. Enjoy it in coffee, hot chocolate, milkshakes, mocktails, or any other creation where a hint of vanilla would elevate the flavor. Indulge in the aromatic and comforting notes of vanilla in your drinks!

Rosemary Simple Syrup

To infuse the herbal flavor of rosemary into simple syrup, you can follow these simple steps:

 **INGREDIENTS**

- 1 cup water
- 1 cup granulated sugar
- 2-3 sprigs of fresh rosemary

 **DIRECTIONS**

1. In a saucepan, combine water and sugar over medium heat. Stir until the sugar has completely dissolved.

2. Once the sugar has dissolved, add the fresh rosemary sprigs to the saucepan. Gently bruise the rosemary by lightly crushing it with the back of a spoon or your fingers. This will help release the essential oils and flavors into your syrup.

3. Let the mixture simmer, gently, over low heat for about 5 minutes, allowing the rosemary to infuse its flavor into the syrup. Stir occasionally.

4. After 5 minutes, remove the saucepan from the heat and let the rosemary-infused syrup cool to room temperature. This allows the flavors to meld and develop.

5. Once cooled, strain the syrup through a fine-mesh sieve or cheesecloth to remove the rosemary sprigs and any small particles. Discard the rosemary solids.

6. Transfer the rosemary-infused syrup to a clean, airtight container, such as a glass bottle or jar, and store it in the refrigerator for up to 1 month.

Now you have your homemade rosemary-infused simple syrup ready to add a touch of herbal goodness to your mocktails or other beverages. It pairs wonderfully with citrus flavors and can bring a delightful twist to your creations. Enjoy the aromatic and savory notes of rosemary in your drinks!

Lavender Simple Syrup

To make lavender simple syrup,
follow these easy steps:

INGREDIENTS

- 1 cup water
- 1 cup granulated sugar
- 2 tablespoons dried culinary lavender buds or 4-5 fresh

lavender sprigs (make sure they are food-grade and free from pesticides)

 DIRECTIONS

1. In a saucepan, combine water and granulated sugar over medium heat.
2. Stir the mixture until the sugar dissolves completely, creating a simple syrup base.
3. Add the dried lavender buds or fresh lavender sprigs to the saucepan.
4. Let the mixture simmer on low heat for about 5 minutes, allowing the lavender to infuse its flavor into the syrup.

5. Remove the saucepan from the heat and let it cool to room temperature, allowing the syrup to steep further.

6. Strain the lavender buds or sprigs from the syrup using a fine mesh strainer or cheesecloth.

7. Transfer the infused lavender simple syrup into a clean glass bottle or jar with a lid.

8. Store the lavender simple syrup in the refrigerator for up to 2 weeks.

Note: You can adjust the strength of the lavender flavor by increasing or decreasing the steeping time. If you prefer a more intense lavender taste, let the lavender steep for a little longer—but be cautious not to over-steep, as many people find an intense lavender taste to be unpleasant or soapy. Prepared properly, Lavender simple syrup is a versatile sweetener that adds a delightful floral essence to a variety of mocktails, cocktails, teas, lemonades, and other beverages. Enjoy experimenting with this fragrant and flavorful syrup in your favorite drinks!

Rose Simple Syrup

To infuse the delicate and floral essence of roses into
simple syrup, you can follow these easy steps:

 **INGREDIENTS**

- 1 cup water
- 1 cup granulated sugar
- 1/4 cup dried rose petals or
  4-6 fresh rose petals (make

sure they are pesticide-
free and suitable for
consumption)

 **DIRECTIONS**

1. In a saucepan, combine water and sugar over medium heat. Stir
   until the sugar has completely dissolved.
2. Once the sugar has dissolved, add the dried or fresh rose petals to
   the saucepan.
3. Bring the mixture to a gentle simmer, stirring occasionally, to allow
   the rose petals to infuse their flavor into the syrup.
4. Let the mixture simmer for about 5 minutes. Be careful not to boil
   the mixture.

5. After simmering, remove the saucepan from the heat and let the rose-infused syrup cool to room temperature. This will allow the flavors to meld and develop.
6. Once cooled, strain the syrup through a fine-mesh sieve or cheesecloth to remove the rose petals and any small particles.
7. Transfer the rose-infused simple syrup to a clean, airtight container, such as a glass bottle or jar, and store it in the refrigerator for up to 1 month.

Now you have your homemade rose-infused simple syrup ready to add a touch of floral sweetness to your beverages. Enjoy it in teas, lemonades, mocktails, or any other creation where the delicate taste of roses can shine. Savor the elegant and fragrant notes of roses in your drinks!

Elderflower Simple Syrup

To make elderflower simple syrup, you can
follow these steps:

 **INGREDIENTS**

- 1 cup water
- 1 cup granulated sugar
- 1/4 cup dried elderflower blossoms or 1/2 cup fresh

elderflower blossoms (pesticide-free, suitable for consumption, cleaned and stems removed)

 **DIRECTIONS**

1. In a saucepan, combine the water and sugar.
2. Heat the mixture over medium heat, stirring constantly, until the sugar dissolves completely.
3. Once the sugar is dissolved, add the dried or fresh elderflower blossoms to the saucepan.
4. Stir the mixture and bring it to a gentle simmer.
5. Allow the mixture to simmer for about 5 minutes to infuse the elderflower flavor into the syrup.

6. Remove the saucepan from the heat and let the syrup cool to room temperature.
7. Once cooled, strain the syrup through a fine-mesh sieve or cheesecloth to remove any flower solids.
8. Transfer the elderflower simple syrup to a clean, airtight container.
9. Store the syrup in the refrigerator for up to two weeks.

Your homemade elderflower simple syrup is now ready to use in a variety of mocktails, adding a delicate floral flavor to your creations. Remember to adjust the amount of syrup used in your mocktails to achieve your desired level of sweetness. Enjoy experimenting with the delightful flavors of elderflower in your mocktail creations!

Chapter 5:

Fruity and Refreshing

SOBER CURIOUS DRINKS

When it comes to non-alcoholic cocktails, fruity and refreshing options are always a hit. These mocktails are bursting with vibrant flavors, tangy citrus notes, and the refreshing essence of fruits. Here are four delightful mocktail recipes to quench your thirst:

Citrus Sunrise

 INGREDIENTS

- 2 oz pineapple juice
- 1 oz orange juice
- 1/2 oz fresh lime juice
- 1/2 oz grenadine syrup (or pomegranate juice mixed with simple syrup)

- Soda water
- Pineapple slice and maraschino cherry, or orange slice for garnish
- Ice cubes

DIRECTIONS

1. Fill a glass with ice cubes.
2. In a shaker, combine the pineapple juice, orange juice, lime juice, and grenadine syrup.
3. Shake well to mix the flavors.
4. Strain the mixture into the glass filled with ice cubes.
5. Top off the glass, to just below the brim, with soda water.
6. Garnish with a pineapple slice and a maraschino cherry on a cocktail pick or orange slices.
7. Serve the Citrus Sunrise and savor the refreshing and tropical combination of pineapple, citrus, and grenadine for a delightful mocktail experience.

Watermelon Mojito

INGREDIENTS

- 1 cup fresh watermelon chunks
- 6-8 fresh mint leaves
- 1 oz lime juice
- 1 oz simple syrup
- Splash of soda water
- Mint sprig and watermelon wedge, for garnish

DIRECTIONS

1. Muddle the watermelon chunks and mint leaves in the bottom of a glass.
2. Add lime juice and simple syrup.
3. Fill the glass with ice cubes.
4. Stir well to combine the flavors.
5. Top with a splash of soda water for a refreshing fizz.
6. Garnish with a mint sprig and a watermelon wedge for an extra touch of freshness.
7. Serve and enjoy on a warm summer day to bring sweet, cooling bliss to your afternoon.

Strawberry Lemon Cooler

 INGREDIENTS

- 2 oz fresh lemon juice
- 1 oz strawberry puree
- 1 oz simple syrup
- 4-6 oz soda water

- Lemon slice and fresh strawberry, for garnish
- Ice cubes

DIRECTIONS

1. Fill a glass with ice cubes.
2. In a shaker, combine the fresh lemon juice, strawberry puree, and simple syrup.
3. Shake well to mix the flavors.
4. Strain the mixture into the glass filled with ice cubes.
5. Top off the glass with soda water.
6. Garnish with a lemon slice and a fresh strawberry on a cocktail pick.
7. Serve the Strawberry Lemon Cooler and relish the tangy and fruity blend of lemon and strawberry in this effervescent mocktail.

Lemon Peach Sparkler

 **INGREDIENTS**

- 1 ripe peach, peeled and pitted
- 1 oz fresh lemon juice
- 1 oz simple syrup
- Soda water
- Fresh mint leaves, for garnish
- Ice cubes

 **DIRECTIONS**

1. In a blender or food processor, puree the ripe peach until smooth.
2. In a glass, combine the peach puree, lemon juice, and simple syrup.
3. Fill the glass with ice cubes.
4. Top it off with soda water, filling the glass to your desired level.
5. Stir gently to combine the flavors.
6. Garnish with fresh mint leaves for a touch of freshness.
7. Sip and enjoy the vibrant and fruity combination of peach and lemon, enhanced by the effervescence of the sparkling water, in this Lemon Peach Sparkler.

These fruity and refreshing mocktails will tantalize your taste buds, transport you to sunny destinations, and keep you feeling relaxed.

Chapter 6:

Herbaceous and Botanical

For those who appreciate the vibrant and aromatic flavors of herbs and botanicals, this category of non-alcoholic cocktails is sure to please. These mocktails showcase the freshness by using herbs like basil, lavender, and rosemary, combined with zesty citrus and other complementary ingredients. Get ready to savor the herbaceous delights of these mocktails!

Cucumber Basil Smash

 INGREDIENTS

- 4–6 cucumber slices, peeled
- 4–6 fresh basil leaves
- 1 oz lime juice
- 1 oz simple syrup

- Splash of soda water
- Cucumber slice and basil sprig, for garnish

 DIRECTIONS

1. In a glass, muddle the cucumber slices and basil leaves to release their flavors.
2. Add lime juice and simple syrup to the glass.
3. Fill the glass with ice cubes.
4. Stir well to combine the ingredients.
5. Top with a splash of soda water for a refreshing fizz.
6. Garnish with a cucumber slice and a sprig of fresh basil.
7. Pair with cooling, summery foods like gazpacho.

Rosemary Grapefruit Spritz

 **INGREDIENTS**

- 2 oz grapefruit juice
- 1 oz rosemary-infused simple syrup
- Splash of soda water
- Grapefruit slice and rosemary sprig, for garnish

DIRECTIONS

1. Fill a glass with ice cubes.
2. Pour grapefruit juice and rosemary-infused syrup into the glass.
3. Stir gently to combine the flavors.
4. Top with a splash of soda water for a refreshing fizz.
5. Garnish with a slice of grapefruit and a sprig of fresh rosemary to elevate the presentation for a backyard cocktail party.

Lavender Berry Fizz

 INGREDIENTS

- 1 oz lavender simple syrup
- 1/2 oz fresh lemon juice
- 4-6 fresh raspberries
- 4-6 fresh blackberries

- Soda water
- Ice cubes
- Fresh lavender sprigs or blackberries, for garnish

 DIRECTIONS

1. In a glass, muddle the fresh raspberries and blackberries to release their juices and flavors.
2. Add the lavender syrup and fresh lemon juice to the glass.
3. Fill the glass with ice cubes.
4. Top it off with soda water, filling the glass to your desired level.
5. Stir gently to mix the ingredients and flavors.
6. Garnish with blackberries or fresh lavender sprigs for an aromatic touch that is sure to soothe your senses.

Lemon Lavender Breeze

 **INGREDIENTS**

- 2 oz lavender simple syrup
- 2 oz fresh lemon juice
- 4-6 oz soda water
- Ice cubes
- Fresh lavender sprigs and lemon slices, for garnish

DIRECTIONS

1. In a shaker, combine the lavender syrup and fresh lemon juice.
2. Fill the shaker with ice cubes and shake well to mix the ingredients.
3. Strain the mixture into a glass filled with fresh ice cubes.
4. Top it off with soda water, filling the glass to your desired level.
5. Stir gently to combine the flavors.
6. Garnish with fresh lavender sprigs and lemon slices for an elegant presentation. The tart acid in this drink will ensure it pairs well with sweet, rich desserts.

These herbaceous and botanical mocktails offer a delightful combination of flavors and aromas that invigorate your senses. Enjoy the harmonious blend of herbs and botanicals, creating a refreshing and sophisticated drinking experience for both yourself and your guests.

Chapter 7:

Creamy and Indulgent

If you're in the mood for a luxurious treat without alcohol, creamy and indulgent mocktails are the way to go. These mocktails offer rich flavors, velvety textures, and a touch of decadence. Indulge yourself with these delightful creations:

Creamy Vanilla Fizz

 INGREDIENTS

- 2 oz vanilla syrup
- 1 oz heavy cream or half-and-half
- 6 oz soda water
- Ice cubes
- Maraschino cherry, for garnish

DIRECTIONS

1. Fill a glass with ice cubes.
2. Pour the vanilla syrup into the glass.
3. Add the heavy cream or half-and-half to the glass.
4. Stir gently to combine the ingredients.
5. Top off the glass with soda water.
6. Garnish with a maraschino cherry on a cocktail pick.
7. Sip and enjoy the nostalgic and creamy flavors of this classic Creamy Vanilla Fizz.

Pineapple Paradise Dream

INGREDIENTS

- 2 oz pineapple juice
- 3 oz canned coconut milk
- 1 oz simple syrup

- Pineapple wedge and maraschino cherry, for garnish
- Ice cubes

DIRECTIONS

1. In a blender, combine the pineapple juice, coconut milk, and simple syrup. Pulse until the mixture is well-incorporated.
2. Add a handful of ice cubes to the blender.
3. Blend on high until all ingredients are well combined and the mixture is smooth.
4. Pour the mocktail into a serving glass.
5. Garnish with a pineapple wedge and a cherry on a cocktail pick.
6. Sip and enjoy the tropical and creamy flavors of this Pineapple Paradise Dream Mocktail.

Coconut Orange Creamsicle

 INGREDIENTS

- 2 oz canned coconut milk
- 3 oz orange juice
- 1 oz vanilla syrup

- Ice cubes
- Orange slice and shredded coconut for garnish

 DIRECTIONS

1. In a blender, combine coconut milk, orange juice, vanilla syrup, and a handful of ice cubes.
2. Blend until smooth and creamy.
3. Pour the mixture into a glass.
4. Garnish with an orange slice and a sprinkle of shredded coconut for a tropical twist.
5. Sip and enjoy the luscious combination of coconut and orange on a hot day. It's excellent for lounging by the pool!

Vanilla Chai Martini

 INGREDIENTS

- 1 cup brewed chai tea (cooled)
- 1/2 cup milk (non-dairy substitutes will work as well)
- 1 oz vanilla simple syrup
- Cinnamon sugar, for rimming the glass
- Ice cubes

DIRECTIONS

1. Rim a martini glass with cinnamon sugar by moistening the rim with water or rubbing it with a slice of lemon, then dipping it into the cinnamon sugar until coated.
2. In a shaker, combine the cooled brewed chai tea, milk, and vanilla simple syrup.
3. Add ice cubes to the shaker and shake well to mix and chill the ingredients.
4. Strain the mixture into the prepared martini glass.
5. Serve the Vanilla Chai Martini and enjoy the comforting blend of aromatic chai tea, creamy milk, and the subtle sweetness of vanilla in this delightful mocktail.

Chapter 8:

Bold and Spicy

The bold and spicy mocktails category is a perfect choice for those who enjoy a kick of bold flavors and a touch of heat. These mocktails feature invigorating combinations of zesty citrus, warming spices, and a peppery kick. Get ready to tantalize your taste buds with these bold and spicy creations:

Spicy Ginger Mule

 INGREDIENTS

- 2 oz fresh lime juice
- 1 oz simple syrup
- 1-inch piece of fresh ginger peeled and thinly sliced
- 4-6 oz ginger brew or ginger ale

- Pinch of cayenne pepper (adjust to taste)
- Ice cubes
- Lime wedges and fresh mint leaves, for garnish

 DIRECTIONS

1. In a shaker, muddle the fresh ginger slices with lime juice and simple syrup to release the ginger's flavors and spice.
2. Add a pinch of cayenne pepper to the shaker and shake well to infuse the spice throughout the mixture.
3. Fill a glass with ice cubes and strain the ginger-lime mixture into the glass.
4. Top it off with ginger brew, filling the glass to your desired level.
5. Stir gently to incorporate the flavors and the effervescence of the ginger beer.
6. Taste the mocktail and adjust the level of cayenne pepper if desired, adding more for extra heat.
7. Garnish with lime wedges and fresh mint leaves for a vibrant presentation. Serve to daring guests with a taste for adventure!

Virgin Bloody Mary

 INGREDIENTS

- 4 oz tomato juice
- 1 oz lemon juice
- 1/2 tsp Worcestershire sauce
- Dash of hot sauce (adjust to taste)
- Pinch of celery salt
- Pinch of black pepper
- Celery stalk and lemon wedge, for garnish

DIRECTIONS

1. Fill a glass with ice cubes.
2. Add tomato juice, lemon juice, Worcestershire sauce, hot sauce, celery salt, and black pepper.
3. Stir well to mix the flavors.
4. Garnish with a celery stalk and a lemon wedge for a classic Bloody Mary presentation.
5. Sip and savor the bold and savory flavors of this spicy mocktail with a weekend brunch.

Ginger Pineapple Blaze

 INGREDIENTS

- 2 oz pineapple juice
- 1 oz lime juice
- 1-inch piece of fresh ginger peeled and thinly sliced
- 1/2 oz simple syrup
- Pinch of cayenne pepper
- Pineapple wedge or lime slice, for garnish
- Ice cubes

DIRECTIONS

1. In a cocktail shaker or mixing glass, add the sliced ginger and simple syrup.
2. Gently muddle the ginger slices to release their flavor and mix with the simple syrup.
3. Add the pineapple juice, lime juice, cayenne pepper, and ice cubes to the shaker.
4. Shake well to combine all the ingredients and chill the mocktail.
5. Strain the mixture into a glass filled with fresh ice cubes.
6. Garnish with a pineapple wedge or lime slice for a tropical touch.
7. Sip and enjoy the fiery blend of tangy pineapple, zesty lime, muddled ginger, and a hint of heat from the cayenne pepper in this Ginger Pineapple Blaze mocktail.

Fireside Cranberry Spice

INGREDIENTS

- 1 cup cranberry juice
- 1/2 cup apple cider
- 1 cinnamon stick
- 2 cloves
- 1 star anise
- 1 tablespoon honey (adjust to taste)
- Orange peel, for garnish

DIRECTIONS

1. In a small saucepan, combine the cranberry juice, apple cider, cinnamon stick, cloves, and star anise.
2. Place the saucepan over low heat and simmer gently for about 10 minutes, allowing the spices to infuse and the flavors to meld.
3. Remove from heat and stir in the honey, adjusting the sweetness to your preference.
4. Strain the mocktail mixture into a heatproof glass or mug.
5. Garnish with a twist of orange peel for an aromatic touch.
6. Sip and savor the comforting and warm blend of cranberry, apple cider, and spices in this delightful Fireside Cranberry Spice Mocktail.

These bold and spicy mocktails will awaken your taste buds and add a fiery kick to your drinking experience. Enjoy the invigorating combination of flavors and spices in each sip.

Chapter 9:

Sophisticated and Elegant

For those seeking a touch of elegance in their non-alcoholic beverages, this category offers refined and elevated mocktails that are sure to impress. With delicate flavors, floral notes, and exquisite presentations, these mocktails are perfect for special occasions or indulging in a sophisticated drink. Enjoy the refined taste of these creations:

Sparkling Raspberry Rose

 INGREDIENTS

- 4-6 fresh raspberries
- 1 oz rose syrup
- 1/2 oz lemon juice

- Soda water
- Edible rose petals, for garnish

 DIRECTIONS

1. In a glass, muddle the fresh raspberries gently to release their flavors.
2. Add rose syrup and lemon juice to the glass.
3. Fill the glass with ice cubes.
4. Top it off with soda water for a refreshing effervescence.
5. Stir gently to combine the ingredients.
6. Garnish with a sprinkle of edible rose petals for an elegant touch.
7. Sip and savor the delicate blend of raspberry and rose flavors.

Here's a tip! Consider freezing rose petals into your ice cubes for a stunning presentation.

Elderflower Spritz

 INGREDIENTS

- 2 oz elderflower syrup
- 1 oz fresh lemon juice
- 4-6 oz soda water
- Ice cubes
- Lemon twists and edible flowers, for garnish

 DIRECTIONS

1. In a glass, combine elderflower syrup and fresh lemon juice.
2. Fill the glass with ice cubes.
3. Top it off with soda water, filling the glass to your desired level.
4. Stir gently to mix the flavors.
5. Garnish with lemon twists and edible flowers for an elegant and whimsical presentation.
6. Sip and savor the delicate floral notes, zesty lemon, and the bubbly effervescence of the soda water in this delightful Elderflower Spritz mocktail.

Cucumber Elder Collins

 INGREDIENTS

- 2 oz cucumber juice (freshly squeezed or store-bought)
- 1 oz elderflower syrup
- 1/2 oz fresh lime juice
- 4-6 oz soda water
- Ice cubes
- Cucumber slices and mint sprigs, for garnish

 DIRECTIONS

1. In a shaker, combine cucumber juice, elderflower syrup, and fresh lime juice.
2. Fill the shaker with ice cubes and shake well to mix the ingredients.
3. Strain the mixture into a glass filled with fresh ice cubes.
4. Top it off with sparkling water or soda, filling the glass to your desired level.
5. Stir gently to incorporate the flavors.
6. Garnish with cucumber slices and mint sprigs for a refreshing and elegant presentation.
7. Sip and enjoy the cool and crisp flavors of cucumber, delicate elderflower, tangy lime, and the effervescence of the sparkling water in this Cucumber Elder Collins mocktail.

Pomegranate Fizz

INGREDIENTS

- 2 oz pomegranate juice
- 1 oz freshly squeezed lime juice
- 1/2 oz simple syrup (adjust to taste)
- 4-6 oz soda water
- Pomegranate arils and lime slice, for garnish
- Ice cubes

DIRECTIONS

1. Fill a glass with ice cubes.
2. In a shaker, combine the pomegranate juice, lime juice, and simple syrup.
3. Shake well to mix the flavors.
4. Strain the mixture into the glass filled with ice cubes.
5. Top off the glass with soda water.
6. Garnish with a few pomegranate arils and a lime slice.
7. Serve the Pomegranate Fizz mocktail and enjoy the refreshing and tangy blend of pomegranate and lime.

These sophisticated and elegant mocktails are perfect for adding a touch of luxury to any occasion. Embrace the refined flavors, exquisite presentations, and the joy of indulging in a creation that exudes elegance.

Chapter 10:

Signature Mocktails from Around the World

Brazilian Caipirinha Mocktail

INGREDIENTS

- 2 oz passion fruit purée
- 1 oz lime juice
- 1 oz simple syrup
- Soda water
- Lime slices, for garnish

DIRECTIONS

1. In a glass, muddle together the lime juice, simple syrup, and passion fruit puree.
2. Fill the glass with ice cubes.
3. Top it off with soda water for a refreshing twist.
4. Stir gently to combine the flavors.
5. Garnish with lime slices for a vibrant and tropical presentation.
6. Sip and enjoy the lively and tangy flavors of this Brazilian-inspired mocktail.

Indian Mango Lassi Twist

 INGREDIENTS

- 1 ripe mango, peeled and diced
- 1 cup plain yogurt (dairy or non-dairy)
- 1/2 cup milk (dairy or non-dairy)
- 1 tbsp honey or maple syrup
- Pinch of cardamom powder
- Mango slice and mint sprig, for garnish

 DIRECTIONS

1. In a blender, combine the diced mango, yogurt, milk, honey or maple syrup, and cardamom powder.
2. Blend until smooth and creamy.
3. Pour the mango lassi into a glass.
4. Garnish with a mango slice and a sprig of fresh mint for an elegant touch.
5. Sip and savor the sweet and tropical flavors of this refreshing Indian-inspired mocktail.

Mexican Agua Fresca de Jamaica

 INGREDIENTS

- 1 cup dried hibiscus flowers
- 4 cups water
- 1/4 cup honey or agave syrup

- 1 lime, juiced
- Lime slices and mint leaves, for garnish

 DIRECTIONS

1. In a saucepan, combine hibiscus flowers and water.
2. Bring to a boil, then reduce heat and simmer for about 10 minutes.
3. Remove from heat and let steep for an additional 10 minutes.
4. Strain the hibiscus tea into a pitcher and discard the flowers.
5. Stir in honey or agave syrup and lime juice until well combined.
6. Chill the agua fresca in the refrigerator.
7. Pour into glasses filled with ice.
8. Garnish with lime slices and mint leaves for a refreshing and vibrant presentation.
9. Sip and enjoy the tart and floral flavors of this Mexican-inspired mocktail.

Italian Bellini Sans Champagne

 INGREDIENTS

- 2 oz peach puree or peach nectar
- 1 oz white grape juice
- 1/2 oz lemon juice
- Soda water
- Peach slice, for garnish

 DIRECTIONS

1. In a glass, combine peach puree or peach nectar, white grape juice, and lemon juice.
2. Fill the glass with ice cubes.
3. Top it off with soda water for a sparkling twist.
4. Stir gently to mix the flavors.
5. Garnish with a peach slice for an elegant and fruity presentation.
6. Sip and savor the delicate and bubbly flavors of this Italian-inspired mocktail, reminiscent of a classic Bellini.

These signature mocktails from around the world capture the essence of their respective cultures and offer a delightful and non-alcoholic experience. Indulge in the unique flavors and embrace the international flair of these mocktails.

Chapter 11:

Dessert-Inspired Mocktails

Indulge your sweet tooth with these delectable dessert-inspired mocktails that offer a delightful twist on classic flavors. From creamy delights to fruity confections, these mocktails bring the joy of dessert to your glass. Whether enjoyed as a refreshing treat on a warm day or as an after-dinner indulgence, these mocktails will satisfy your dessert cravings.

Strawberry Shortcake Fizz

 INGREDIENTS

- 4-6 fresh strawberries
- 1 oz fresh lemon juice
- 1 oz vanilla simple syrup
- Soda water

- Fresh strawberries, for garnish
- Ice cubes

 DIRECTIONS

1. In a glass, muddle the fresh strawberries with the lemon juice and vanilla simple syrup to release their juices and flavors.
2. Fill the glass with ice cubes.
3. Top it off with soda water, filling the glass to your desired level.
4. Stir gently to combine the flavors.
5. Garnish with fresh strawberries for an inviting presentation.
6. Sip and savor the refreshing and fruity combination of muddled strawberries, tangy lemon, and the effervescence of the soda water in this Strawberry Shortcake Fizz mocktail.

Chocolate Mint Frost

 INGREDIENTS

- 1 scoop vanilla ice cream (dairy or non-dairy)
- 2 oz milk (dairy or non-dairy)
- 1/4 oz mint extract
- 1/2 oz chocolate syrup
- A handful of chocolate chips
- Whipped cream and chocolate shavings, for garnish

 DIRECTIONS

1. In a blender, combine the vanilla ice cream, milk, mint extract, and chocolate syrup.
2. Blend until smooth and creamy.
3. Add the chocolate chips and pulse briefly to incorporate them.
4. Pour the shake into a glass.
5. Top with a dollop of whipped cream and sprinkle with chocolate shavings for an indulgent finish.

Dreamy Java Delight

 INGREDIENTS

- 1 scoop vanilla ice cream (dairy or non-dairy)
- 1/2 oz chocolate syrup
- 1 oz strong brewed coffee, cooled

- 1 oz milk (dairy or non-dairy)
- Whipped cream
- Chocolate shavings or cocoa powder, for garnish

 DIRECTIONS

1. Drizzle the inside of a glass with chocolate syrup, creating a swirl pattern.
2. In a blender, combine the cooled brewed coffee, milk, and vanilla ice cream.
3. Add a handful of ice cubes to the blender and blend on high speed until the mixture is smooth and creamy.
4. Pour the mocktail mixture into the prepared glass, filling it about three-quarters full.
5. Top with a dollop of whipped cream and sprinkle chocolate shavings or cocoa powder over the whipped cream for garnish.
6. Serve the Creamy Java Delight Mocktail immediately with a straw or a long spoon for stirring.
7. Sip and enjoy the indulgent flavors of chocolate and coffee in this creamy and decadent Mocktail.

Peachy Cream Bliss

 **INGREDIENTS**

- 2 oz peach puree
- 2 oz milk (dairy or non-dairy)
- 1 oz vanilla syrup
- 1 oz coconut cream
- Peach slice, for garnish
- Crushed graham crackers, for garnish
- Ice cubes

 **DIRECTIONS**

1. In a blender, combine the peach puree, milk, vanilla syrup, and coconut cream.
2. Blend until smooth and creamy.
3. Fill a glass with ice cubes.
4. Pour the creamy mixture over the ice.
5. Garnish with a peach slice on the rim of the glass.
6. Sprinkle crushed graham crackers on top for a touch of texture and sweetness.
7. Serve the Creamy Peach Dream mocktail and savor the luscious combination of creamy coconut, sweet peach, and a hint of vanilla.

These dessert-inspired mocktails offer a sweet ending to any meal or a work as a delightful treat on their own. Sip and enjoy the flavors of your favorite desserts in a refreshing and non-alcoholic form.

Chapter 12:

Fruity & Tangy Shrub Bases

Now that you have a basis for mixing mocktails, it's time to enhance your skills by using tangy and fruity shrubs in your drinks.

In the context of beverages, a shrub refers to a type of syrup made from a combination of fruit, sugar, and vinegar. It is a flavorful and tangy mixture that can add depth and complexity to cocktails and mocktails.

The process of making a shrub involves macerating or mashing fresh fruit with sugar to extract its juices and create a sweet base. This mixture is then combined with vinegar, which provides the shrub with its distinctive tanginess and acts as a natural preservative.

Shrubs originated as a way to preserve fruits before refrigeration was widely available. The combination of sugar and vinegar helps to preserve the flavors and extend the shelf life of the fruit mixture.

Shrubs come in various flavors and can be made using different fruits, such as berries, citrus, or tropical fruits, combined with various types of vinegar. The resulting syrup can be stored for an extended period and used to enhance the flavors of beverages.

In addition to being used in drinks, shrubs can also be used as a flavorful ingredient in salad dressings, marinades, and even desserts. Their unique sweet and tangy flavor profile adds a refreshing and complex element to various culinary creations.

Overall, a shrub is a versatile syrup that can elevate the taste of your beverages and culinary creations, offering a balance of sweetness and tanginess to enhance the overall flavor profile of any gastro-creation.

Here are three flavorful shrub recipes that can be used as a base in mocktails.

Strawberry Basil Shrub

To make a refreshing Strawberry Basil shrub,
follow these simple steps:

 INGREDIENTS

- 1 cup fresh strawberries, hulled and sliced
- 1 cup granulated sugar
- 1 cup apple cider vinegar
- 1/4 cup fresh basil leaves, torn

 DIRECTIONS

1. In a bowl, combine the sliced strawberries and sugar. Mix well to coat the strawberries with sugar. Let the mixture sit for about 10-15 minutes to allow the sugar to draw out the juices from the strawberries.
2. After the strawberries have released their juices, add the torn basil leaves to the bowl. Gently muddle the basil leaves with the strawberries using a muddler or the back of a spoon. This will help release the flavors and aromas of the basil.
3. Pour the strawberry mixture into a clean glass jar or container, then add the apple cider vinegar. Stir well to combine all the ingredients.

4.   Seal the jar tightly and let it sit at room temperature for 24 to 48 hours. During this time, the flavors will meld together, and the vinegar will extract the essence of the strawberries and basil.

5.   After resting, strain the shrub mixture through a fine-mesh sieve or cheesecloth into a clean bottle or jar. This removes the solids and leaves you with a smooth and flavorful shrub.

6.   Store the Strawberry Basil shrub in the refrigerator for up to several months. The flavors will continue to develop over time, so feel free to taste and adjust the sweetness or acidity as desired.

Now you have a homemade Strawberry Basil shrub ready to be used in your mocktails. Experiment with different combinations and enjoy the unique and tangy flavor profile that this shrub brings to your beverages.

Pineapple Ginger Shrub

To make a delightful Pineapple Ginger shrub,
follow these simple steps:

 **INGREDIENTS**

- 2 cups fresh pineapple, diced
- 1 cup granulated sugar
- 1 cup apple cider vinegar

- 1-inch piece of fresh ginger, peeled and thinly sliced

 DIRECTIONS

1. In a saucepan, combine the diced pineapple, sugar, and ginger slices. Stir well to ensure the sugar coats the pineapple and ginger evenly.

2. Place the saucepan over medium heat and cook the mixture, stirring occasionally, until the sugar has dissolved and the pineapple begins to release its juices. This process usually takes about 5-7 minutes.

3. Once the mixture starts to simmer and the pineapple has softened, remove the saucepan from the heat and let it cool for a few minutes.

4. Transfer the cooked pineapple and ginger mixture into a clean glass jar or container. Add the apple cider vinegar and stir well to combine.

5. Seal the jar tightly and let it sit at room temperature for 24 to 48 hours. This resting period allows the flavors to infuse and develop.

6. After the resting period, strain the shrub mixture through a fine-mesh sieve or cheesecloth into a clean bottle or jar. This will remove solids and leave you with a smooth and flavorful shrub.

7. Store the Pineapple Ginger shrub in the refrigerator for up to several months. The flavors will continue to develop and mellow over time, so feel free to adjust for taste as the flavor profile develops.

Now you have a homemade Strawberry Basil shrub ready to be used in your mocktails. Experiment with different combinations and enjoy the unique and tangy flavor profile that this shrub brings to your beverages.

Raspberry Rosemary Shrub

To make a delicious Raspberry Rosemary
shrub, follow these simple steps:

INGREDIENTS

- 2 cups fresh raspberries
- 1 cup granulated sugar
- 1 cup apple cider vinegar
- 2 sprigs of fresh rosemary

DIRECTIONS

1. In a bowl, combine the raspberries and sugar. Gently mash the raspberries with a fork or muddler to release their juices and mix them with the sugar.
2. Add the rosemary sprigs to the bowl and lightly bruise them with a muddler or the back of a spoon to release their aroma.
3. Transfer the raspberry and rosemary mixture into a clean glass jar or container. Pour the apple cider vinegar over the mixture.
4. Stir well to ensure the sugar is dissolved and the ingredients are well combined.

5. Seal the jar tightly and let it sit at room temperature for 24 to 48 hours. During this time, the flavors will infuse, and the vinegar will extract the essence of the raspberries and rosemary.

6. After resting, strain the shrub mixture through a fine-mesh sieve or cheesecloth into a clean bottle or jar. This removes the solids and leaves you with a smooth and flavorful shrub.

7. Store the Raspberry Rosemary shrub in the refrigerator for up to several months. The flavors will continue to develop over time, so feel free to taste and adjust the sweetness or acidity as desired.

Now you have a homemade Raspberry Rosemary shrub ready to add a tangy and herbaceous twist to your mocktails. Experiment with different combinations and enjoy the unique flavor profile that this shrub brings to your beverages.

Chapter 13:

Tangy Shrub Mocktails

Next, let's explore four delicious mocktail recipes you can create with your homemade shrubs to add a unique and tangy twist to your drinks:

Tangy Shrub Spritz

 INGREDIENTS

- 2 oz shrub of your choice (such as raspberry rosemary, pineapple ginger, or strawberry basil)

- 3 oz soda water
- Fresh herbs or fruit slices, for garnish

 DIRECTIONS

1. Fill a glass with ice cubes.
2. Pour the shrub over the ice.
3. Top it off with soda water for a light and refreshing effervescence.
4. Stir gently to blend the flavors.
5. Garnish with fresh herbs or fruit slices for an elegant touch.
6. Sip and savor the unique combination of the shrub's tangy notes and the soda water's crispness.

Strawberry Basil Shrub Sparkler

 **INGREDIENTS**

- 1 oz strawberry basil shrub
- 1/2 oz lime juice
- Soda water

- Fresh strawberries, lime slice, and basil leaves, for garnish

 **DIRECTIONS**

1. In a glass, combine the strawberry basil shrub and lime juice.
2. Fill the glass with ice cubes.
3. Top it off with soda water for a sparkling base.
4. Stir gently to mix the flavors.
5. Garnish with fresh strawberries, lime slice, and basil leaves for an elegant presentation.
6. Sip and enjoy the delightful combination of tangy strawberries, aromatic basil, and effervescent soda water.

Pineapple Ginger Shrub Punch

 INGREDIENTS

- 1 oz pineapple ginger shrub
- 2 oz pineapple juice
- 1/2 oz lime juice
- Ginger ale

- Pineapple wedges and crystallized ginger, for garnish

 DIRECTIONS

1. In a shaker, combine the pineapple ginger shrub, pineapple juice, and lime juice.
2. Shake well with ice.
3. Strain the mixture into a glass filled with fresh ice cubes.
4. Top it off with ginger ale for a refreshing fizz.
5. Stir gently to combine the flavors.
6. Garnish with pineapple wedges and a piece of crystallized ginger for a tropical touch.
7. Sip and savor the tangy-sweet flavors of pineapple, zesty ginger, and the effervescence of the ginger ale.

Raspberry Rosemary Shrub Sour

INGREDIENTS

- 1 oz raspberry rosemary shrub
- 1/2 oz lemon juice
- 1/2 oz simple syrup
- Soda water
- Fresh raspberries, and rosemary sprig or mint, for garnish

DIRECTIONS

1. In a glass, combine the raspberry rosemary shrub, lemon juice, and simple syrup.
2. Fill the glass with ice cubes.
3. Top it off with soda water for a bubbly base.
4. Stir gently to blend the flavors.
5. Garnish with fresh raspberries and a sprig of rosemary or mint for an elegant presentation.
6. Sip and enjoy the tangy raspberries, aromatic rosemary, and the sparkling effervescence of this delightful mocktail.

These mocktail recipes demonstrate how shrubs can add depth and complexity to your alcohol-free beverages. Experiment with different fruit and herb combinations to create your own unique shrub-based mocktails.

Chapter 14:

Host A Non-Alcoholic Cocktail Party

It's time to celebrate your sober curious journey!

Hosting a mocktail party is a wonderful opportunity to bring friends, family, and loved ones together to enjoy a festive and alcohol-free gathering. Whether it's a special occasion or simply a casual get-together, creating a memorable mocktail party involves planning, creative touches, and a welcoming ambiance. In this chapter, we will guide you and provide suggestions for you to host a successful and enjoyable party.

When developing a mocktail menu for your party, select options that offer a variety of flavors and styles to cater to different preferences. Include a mix of fruity, herbal, creamy, and bold mocktails to ensure there is something for everyone.

You can be the mixologist and make drinks for everyone or set up a DIY mocktail bar. Setting up a DIY mocktail bar provides your party with an interactive and creative element, allowing guests to personalize their beverages according to their taste preferences.

Here's how to set up a DIY Mocktail Bar:

- Designate a dedicated area as your DIY mocktail bar. It can be a separate table or a designated space on the kitchen counter.

- Arrange the necessary ingredients and tools for guests to create their mocktails. Include a variety of mocktail bases, syrups, fresh fruits, herbs, garnishes, mixers, and ice.

- Provide an assortment of glassware, including highball glasses, martini glasses, and tumblers, along with stirring spoons, muddlers, shakers, and strainers.

- Display recipe cards or a menu with mocktail ideas and suggested ingredient combinations to inspire guests' creations.

- Ensure you have enough ice buckets, tongs, and plenty of ice to keep the mocktail bar well-stocked throughout the event. And don't forget a decorative tub where guests can dispose of used utensils so that the preparation area stays clean.

Mocktail Bases and Mixers:

- Offer a selection of mocktail bases that serve as the foundation for guests' creations. These can include options such as fruit juices (orange, cranberry, pineapple), flavored syrups (vanilla, rosemary, lavender), or infused water (cucumber, mint, lemon).

- Provide a range of mixers like soda water, ginger ale, and lemon-lime soda to add fizz and enhance the flavors of the mocktails.

Fresh Fruits, Herbs, and Garnishes:

- Offer a vibrant assortment of fresh fruits and herbs that guests can use to enhance their mocktails. Include options like sliced citrus fruits (lemons, limes, oranges), berries (strawberries, raspberries, blackberries), cucumber slices, and mint sprigs.

- Set out various garnishes such as sugar for sugar rims, edible flowers, cocktail picks, and colorful straws to add a decorative touch to the mocktails.

Mocktail and Appetizer Pairings:

- Pairing mocktails with complementary appetizers enhances the overall experience and creates a harmonious balance of flavors. Here are some pairing suggestions from the book:

- Fruity and Refreshing: Pair a Citrus Sunrise mocktail with a platter of fresh fruit skewers or a watermelon and feta salad.

- Herbaceous and Botanical: Serve a Cucumber Basil Smash mocktail with cucumber and dill finger sandwiches or a goat cheese and herb crostini.

- Creamy and Indulgent: Pair a Pineapple Paradise Dream with coconut shrimp or mini mango cheesecakes.

- Bold and Spicy: Serve a Spicy Ginger Mule mocktail with chicken wings or stuffed jalapeño poppers.

- Sophisticated and Elegant: Pair an Elderflower Spritz with smoked salmon canapés or brie and fig bruschetta.

- Dessert-Inspired: Serve a Strawberry Shortcake Fizz with mini chocolate-covered strawberries or bite-sized cheesecake bites.

Personalization and Guidance:

- Encourage guests to get creative and experiment with different combinations of ingredients. Offer guidance and suggestions if guests need inspiration or assistance in creating their mocktails.

- Have a knowledgeable helper available at the mocktail bar to answer questions, provide recommendations, and assist with any technical aspects, such as muddling or shaking.

Decor and Presentation:

- Decorate the mocktail bar area with themed decorations that match the party's overall aesthetic. Consider using colorful tablecloths, fresh flowers, or signage displaying mocktail-related quotes or instructions.

- Use labeled jars, bottles, or trays to organize the ingredients and garnishes neatly. Consider adding decorative accents like string lights or a customized mocktail bar sign.

By setting up a DIY mocktail bar, you empower your guests to become their own mixologists, fostering creativity and engagement while providing a memorable and interactive experience. Encourage guests to explore different flavors, share their creations, and enjoy the process of crafting personalized mocktails. Remember to have fun and celebrate the joy of mocktail mixology with your guests. Cheers to a successful DIY mocktail bar experience!

AUTHOR'S NOTE

I was inspired to write this book while on my own sober curious journey. While giving up alcohol, I missed the taste of a fancy, flavorful drink at the end of my day or while hanging out with friends.

The recipes in this book helped me to replace my unhealthy alcohol addiction without feeling deprived, having a raging hangover, or waking up with regrets in the morning.

I hope these recipes spark joy for you, as well, while you discover new drinks to relax and entertain you along your sober curious journey.

To learn more about the sober curious movement, check out Ruby Warrington's book, *"The Sober Curious Reset: Change the Way You Drink in 100 Days or Less."*

If you enjoyed this book, please leave a review to help other sober curious people who are considering giving this incredible journey a go. I would love to hear about your favorite recipe from this book or the recipe you are most excited to try in your review!

Thank you for reading.

With gratitude,

Stella Rose Wilder

INDEX

Made in the USA
Las Vegas, NV
10 December 2023

82503886R00056